Other Clues

Other books by Grace Marie Grafton:

Visiting Sisters

Zero (Winner of the Poetic Matrix Press chapbook contest)

Other Clues

poems by

Grace Marie Grafton

Latitude Press
Pittsburg, California

Previously published:

Omnidawn Blog: Evidence, Embrace (published as "The Ungrieved World"), Unsaid (published as "Language is how ghosts enter the world")

Edgz: Worship (I)

Printed in the United States of America

ISBN 978-0-9819534-3-4
Library of Congress Control Number 2010921386

Published by
Latitude Press, imprint of RAW ArT PRESS
www.rawartpress.com
Trena Machado, Publisher

Front cover, original painting, *Angels and Taxidermy:*
  Brianna Johnson Smeds
Drawings, pages 18, 24, 36, 42, 50, 62, 68, 74, 80:
  Brianna Johnson Smeds

Cover Design: Inez Machado
Photo back cover: Michael Grafton

Acknowledgments

In writing *Other Clues,* I received much inspiration from reading the poems of other poets, and from viewing artwork by some of my favorite artists. I wish to acknowledge their contribution to my creativity. I especially thank the following poets, James Tate, W. S. Merwin, Anne Michaels, and Rumi (Coleman Barks, translator); the painters, Joyce Treiman, Edgar Degas, Wassily Kandinsky; the sculptor, Lazlo Fekete.

A heartfelt thank you to Brianna Johnson Smeds for her beautiful art; she is a dear and valued member of my family. Thank you to my loving husband, Michael Grafton, for his support of my poetry and, with this book, his invaluable help with anything to do with computers. Many thanks to Trena Machado, my patient, perceptive editor. Thank you to Rusty Morrison, Melissa Kwasny, Barbara Joan Tiger-Bass, and my long-time poetry group for their continuing support of my poetry.

CONTENTS

Quarter Notes

The Experienced Bride

The Inadvisable

There is no scatheless rapture.

Charles Frazier

Quarter Notes

Allure

She started young to build her amiable solitude, orbit of smile in the pluralistic undergrowth. Sorrel, checkerplant, her dynamic companions. Candles in evening music, her breath devising tender messages no one hears.

She has cared for plural, the quill to write X loves Y into the record of days, but when the umbilicus could not leave off quarreling with blood that stained the birth bed, silence under leaves lent her heart habit.

She hasn't given up. Neither will she pursue the mirror moment.

Fashioning a figure of her future, she curves the green line back on its start, threads it through fingers and hair, evening's orange hour.

Self-portrait in quarter notes

A knack for the versatile melody, when she boards the ship, her satchel of words slips over the railing and snuggles serenely into mindless waves. Her steps wager balance, pineal gland her compass.

The years she frets over the litter under her house of soul, the crow caws batter her foundation, insist she paint it no color any artist has previously used. Listening to their bogus logic loses her amulet. She's left with the lackluster of everyday stairs.

Pincushion will never be her artifact, she hands needles and pins to Grandma in the barter over identity. Oxford shoes are out but she wants ribbons, for her young years anyway. Metal frying pans, recipe for pickles, Mother's midnight-blue Chinese dragon robe, even though it's torn.

Arpeggios of purpose plague her, why not pray for clearer instincts, more like the sowbug or wolverine. She moves not easily forward or sideways, there's always the abstracting glint. Her heart follows sidereal harmonies.

Grandchild

Coached in ways to lure ornate beetles to the shoreline of her concentrated questions, she places a coin on the path to draw interference elsewhere, simple lore being better, a truer measure of beetle intensity. Her mind's landscape resembles the fairy tales that sing babies to sleep. Behind the number eight, she stores encyclopedic characterizations of starting points. She won't discount rumor, keeps climbing ladders to Great Grandma's attic. Nothing nailed down, the fraying tablecloths redeem the practice of needlework, recipes without peer. She links beetle to star, inaudible guide up ragged redwood bark that squirrels, in spring, tear off in great hunks.

Destiny

A burlap sack filled with words that are the seeds of ideas, when the child wishes only for pieces of hard candy. Shrewd, she could sell the ones she doesn't eat, for twice what the mothers expect to pay, if she can carry them to the far side of town—the trim foliage, the hunger for foreign rumor. It's too late.

Her fate is not to be sweet but scholarly. Who will ever witness her pragmatic nature, her willingness to labor, to shortcut down alleys, despite feral dogs?

What was promised at her birth is not her fault, her mind now at the western border, her dream dead. She's ready to cross the bridge that will separate her from her mother, the melt of skin and breasts. "Fly away," her mother waves, "Yellow leads you, forget consonant blue." What might she weave with her words, how might she sew them to the sun?

The reason the three mice are called blind

The way the child wants desperately, brightly, to answer any imponderable question, displaying blatantly her fear of crossing into unconquerable territory her sister entered. Before she was six years old, starting to make sense of the world, and envied Sister's grip on dimensions she herself could not understand. Then serious bewilderment: a lost sister, disappearance of the accountable outlines she had woo'd into place. The one who helped her understand differences between days, months, weeks. Together they were diggers who discovered *real*, *unreal*, which one would hold you when you cried. That Saturday morning over the backyard fence, hide 'n seek, someone went too far. The nettle patch, the camping lantern they weren't supposed to mess with, daytime stars on water close up, nighttime stars too far to touch. Who had waylaid her sister, snatched her into a fairy-tale tower? If she could find it, could she drum signals on the base, open a magic door, name the enchanted name?

Existenz

Hard to tell the truth. She wants to but the prickle over her scalp. Past truth was, for her, the lamb to the slaughter. The three best chrysanthemums stolen from sidewalk yards, presented it's true for the sake of a smile, pencil to the student of the day. "Sorry, sorry," she mutters, knowing her father and attempting to weasel out of anything she's ever said, sweep her truth under the rug, that became the (surreptitious) engagement to the bottle. Visit to the zoo where nouns and verbs were tertiary if not nothing. She holds a candle to the calendar, half of the days burn into a mad tango on the downhill slope.

The loss

Her raga of discontent, hosanna of puerile self-love. Haggle as she might with the Queen of Hearts, "Oh please, a presence with gravitas rather than simper," she's not allowed to steal her destiny. The populace will laud her, then castigate. She'll have to wear see-through over a silk bodysuit, no humility. Paparazzi will spy, there'll be no brother to turn to. She could have cast spells with the candle before it got lost but thought herself too young to interfere with prescience. Now only her shadowy backyard on moon-free nights will hide her from all who swear they love her.

Flight

Flag-thought and the empty-cupboard congeal into a coincidence of escalators except she eschews mechanics and follows only the furniture of "summer comes after spring."

Between confetti shower and deeper concentration, her stanza cannot hold.

She pares it down to six questions, beginning with the difference between mourners. Do they weave and bob to box loss's dictates? Or do they circle and circle with the flying swallow, viewing ever wider the converse of their personal day? Territory dwindles.

But the air, oh!

Is she learning to fall?

Journey

She relinquishes control in order to stay on the path that won't perish in willows' upscale growth. Beauty flaunted to frogs, owls with versatile midnight sights, coyotes upslope in cliff's secret. Flip the coin can't guarantee wealth's serenade under her mullioned window or diva diving into swimming pool intervals. *Random* seems to be her Prince Charming. Tattered satin, beaded moccasins, his waltz now more a tired jig, but the accordion still rattles out the polka and the zither thrums sounds of unplanted field grass outside the city limits.

She blurts out, "I'm lost."

I never had the chance to unpack. I've misplaced my guide and cannot halt until some sign—lamp in a window, ivory relic dropped on a sidewalk. Might ease the traces of past shoddiness, the way I clung even to the ragged pillow. I search, though slowly now, for a tree I could recognize as the one I dreamed or read about in Grandma's hymnal. But I couldn't have read it, it was in her native tongue. I arrive at snow's edge, spring run-off divulging music for which I have no instrument. Spongy ground, last season's needles, not the kind whose eye no camel could pass through.

Accustomed travel

She uses the same suitcase, the trip to Athens as well as the trip to Missoula, although contrasting weather might have suggested otherwise. They say promises are made to be broken, but she's careful not to let the door hinges squeak when she steals out to sleep in the barn. The stag's head mounted on the big support beam, cheap child's trumpet hanging from its antlers, a lack she snuggles into. Which parade does she belong to, which celebration fits her skin? When she was young, it was the limb of the oak tree, line up of acorns, all their miniature cups. Oh melancholy regard, old phonograph she keeps in the hayloft, Bach's violin partitas performing open-heart healing. She lolls in the hammock, hoping owl droppings don't land on her, hope buoyed by the lilt left in a barn empty of any domestic animals.

In full wing again

When autobiographical details compose their own still life.

Sombrero plays the harmonica in the left back corner.

Time to introduce fallible mornings to each other. July in the mountains. Waterfall buries her betrayal under rocks heedlessly thrown. Heads still in the gauze of innocence. Where does her wit fit? Or the movies her mother cast her in? The clock Father set out to snare birds of paradise. The No-No Flowers oddly beautiful on World War II stems. Grandma's crocheted shawl hiding the disappeared Japanese neighbors.

How to revise the insistencies, make the family more Madison Avenue? That black and white photo of Prague as the backdrop: tank, gun barrel, corpses' dark blood puddling. Bertolt Brecht and Kurt Weil dolls wear trumpets and accordions to perplex the soundtrack.

There's vacancy toward the center where gold ore melts itself continually into transparent jugs that spill and chatter.

The Experienced Bride

Wishes, lies

The problem even before I send out the invitations will be to thaw
the lake before the waning moon starts to fret.

Why aren't rising profits more tempting? Instead, I get advice over
the loudspeaker regarding my grubstake.

I wasn't the last one in the lady's room the night the pulse started to
wave through 1:00 A.M.'s jumpsuit, but the kiss was as provable as
anybody's and it was mine. My ass on the line to wrap up doubt, the
combination safe no thing could rip apart.

Still, I want what I can't have: that my nephew's lyrics won't separate
me from prayer, that dead honeybees leave their hexagons behind for
study, that final clues retain their repartee.

Leave-taking

In four days, the scrapbook will be handed down. We stand on the balcony, thin moon eschewing correctness, its normal night course failing the premonitions day gathers from faint edges.

I've propped my expectations against the railing, I try not to recall the first-marriage opera, whinging skeleton-baby in the back closet that threatens my sense of trust whenever tendrils appear.

Small-town gossipy mind back at my prom dress, my sprawling ambition I wouldn't atone for even when Fair Chance on its white horse gleamed aslant my digressions.

I shove the scrapbook into Prince Charming's hands, lift him with me, over the railing. Floating downstream now, my ankles flutter in what buoys me: parallel path to lipstick, to coif, to the hive of murky promise.

Impossible endings

To begin with *Z* as in zero is to beggar instructions, the way, young, we thought the end was a circus trick. We went about needing to learn how to tie our shoes and come out of the creek before our lips turned blue. Time tightens its unbearable hand around our brows the more we understand the word "after," the more seriously we iron creases into our slacks. I know my eyes are tired, woman now condemned to short division, but consider the design in the peacock's tail, center blue whose notch projects me beyond grief. The ardent green second circle a premise that listens unbelievingly to the impossible flight. How could anyone expect this heavy-tailed bird would be blessed with such fortune?

Dis-order

Close the armload of books on self-improvement, take the laundry across the footbridge. Nearer the stream, rocks whistle a lullaby.

I can't introduce my wash into the watershed, never mind former habits. Quail calls crackle along the circles sun leaves among berry brambles. I counsel myself to stop complaining and take for granted I'll never be safe.

Agile, my wish to stitch family into my wanderings, bring all my here's and there's into the underbrush. Leave the lilac gardens to East Coast order. It seems my worn socks, my slept-in sheets will be wrung by rain, hung in the interstices of thimbleberry and vetch.

Forgive myself the twigs in my boots, remove conscience's cover from my hymnbook, the psalm lays me down in green graves.

I could be worth the attendant inchworms.

Meditation

I sit on the bench made of crowns before it collapses.

Sunset mummifies day, what a jumble, river water pink solace, vehicle
for the wholly ordained.

Hawks nest in oak limbs near my forehead, I have to shut up or lose
them though I know they'll be noisy.

Summer heat cedes night's spaces, I cede my Texas border, prefer the
blue heron but she's a winter bird, conduit of necessary change.

Impulse

The red room was a first dream, a way to place a banner anyone could understand. Nothing eternal of course, walls can always be altered. My mind travels to the moon's autumn hue or that awkward mauve I could never explain. I fish out the worn interior-decorator justification: personal whim and the dollars to make one's past faux pas recede behind a new antique screen. Refusal to be enslaved by consistency, whose visage I consign to the sticker patch behind Dad's orange grove. I'm mortal, I use what vehicle I can to haul my walls into the shimmer that matches molecules dashing about my blood's luster. I know, even they are harnessed to eventual non-identity but: a present salon in my living room, conversation on the rim of darkness, echo of planets' ghostly presence.

Leaching the acorns

I won't say, "Bait my humor," but combat boots are embarrassing especially when essential children ask me about swinging on eucalyptus trees.

My quarrel with the white dinner veil puts laughter in the cupboard while sugarcane molders in the fields.

Crickets won't accept my itinerary for an answer, their weather supplies the phase they need, evening's commonness.

Please turn on the entertainment, I've been soaking in the war too long.

Though it's autumn, my pampered notions think, "Spring up/run away."

My mother made play dates, wasn't all laundry and potato peels for her, she knew to throw the baby out of the bath water. Dad was a pacifist.

Complaint

Nineteen ninety-one and the clock is a gift conniving time's beggar to climb the rope fastened to the colt who can't yet carry a saddle.

Lipstick on the doorjamb conceals where the chisel left its scar when the former owner departed before the sod could rise up and tangle him in its monopoly.

The full moon's grimace leaves us dissatisfied, we're ready to heave Thanksgiving out of the corner the material turkey trapped it in, victim of laissez-faire's mythology. Slice off a feather to tickle the sharp-shooter's nose before the sky falls into the festivities and embarrasses dutiful *pleases* and *thank yous*.

Don't we know babies can leverage the truth out of especially mamas before their gaze goes all cagy, stinking down the halls of power?

Blessed hearts, bleeding and kneeling, paying too many pennies for any thought.

Swallowing fast

The smell of amber imbricates the room's air. It states, "I waft a former epoch among the steadfast Present." New sap each spring, each day an erasure. Faster and faster people's nostalgia for lost memories. Floating toward any upcoming medical miracle, a laser knife that could contradict our infatuation with speed by moving so slowly it persuades only the tumor that life is not worth living. The knife knows to leave healthy tissues alone. Echoes of the Philippines' "psychic" surgeons but, old-fashioned as they are, they feel they must show bloody evidence—the "removed" symptom. Jesus and Lazarus. Who knows? But no one can deny that newspapers get burned to ignite hearth fires and line the shoes of the homeless. Our news quickly old, our faces turn again to the east, the west, south, north, up. Not behind, not down.

How many stories are the jewelry of the world?

Sojourning maiden climbs to the treetop, would-be safe canopy, only to have the mythical wolf with the question-mark tail climb after her and eat her into the sleeve of night. The exiled family wrapped in gauzy fog, led by the fox who blows a tin whistle and guides them into the calculus of rescue. How would they fit their ragged selves into his den? But *real* doesn't enter *story*. Mind's power: osmosis—cellular explosion. The queen mother wears the apple crown, lacquers her hair with wind. Open the lid of her box, drink her syrup of *answer*. Always the chance of kissing in the hedge, reaching back into fossil time. We know what kissing promises, what most stories intimately tell. Bring down the pictures from the attic, regard the radiant faces. Reveal serious escapes.

Other clues

She tastes the flavors of doors opening or his eyes a spoon's rattle in the Haviland cup. What was it her mother said, "Always look at the bottom?" Bringing Mama that dragon cup from Chinatown was wrong. Look in the back of the tourist shops for hand-embroidered silk animals or tissue-paper art carefully cut. The amethyst, jade, the carnelian beads. She doesn't have to listen to the drunk's words to know, to avoid knowing. She just reads for sound, music her mind lifts into and the rush of red-like legs in Lampo Leong's paintings of Light and Gravity. Understanding's a grave matter and the light in the body, the way she can say, "Light in the body" though she knows there is no light there. The way the body belongs in space, thoughts of air escape while feet maintain a tie with gravity. The look in his eyes, grave as the darkness that holds her tenderly, his hands in the night on her body. She does not define words he speaks, they're part of the light in her mind.

Worship (I)

The interval for learning to fly expired before the news on my radar re-marked my attention, wrapped in whether the fuchsia would bloom this particular summer. I worship the notion of going beyond humanity's entrenched subscription to the law of gravity. Not failing to realize the fuchsia would never bloom in outer space, that's not the flying I have in mind. More like levitation. Runnel through near associations, redwood groves or out into the canyon's groove above coast oaks. A bubble unnoticed by birds. Idle cloud stitching my way. How I float in a lake waiting with no sense of *wait*. Why do anything? Except, hunger would force me to descend. I don't want to shed my arms, don't want to be inhuman. Maybe that's why I missed the deadline. I'm not dead.

The moves

Is there any pause between the ways I change my seeing, current
flowing below the current window?

All this pointless consideration when lost buttons need to be found
and re-sewn into the socket they were made for.

The whirr of the first sewing machine (to make life easier) shown in
jerky film. Silent near the beginning of invention, before sound became
extrapolated from its origins, hoof beats provided by coconut shells.

Mundane urban spectrum grays out sunset's apricot hues.

What am I to do with imagination but create a studio where buttons
approximate orchid's ovaries and I invent indoor grass?

The unpin-able

Yesterday basked over a party where incantation jostled propriety.

Everyone wishes for revelation before elevation. Read the instructions:
NO LAUNDRY WASHING HERE.

Over there briny minds pickle the snobbish hats of materialism's reign.

The noumenal in pink underwear, frivolous, ribald, easy to toss back
with a chaser.

It isn't a parade in rhythmical starboard, it's the unpin-able nucleus
slipping an eye through the expandable territory of its own molecule.

No appeasement in the epochal cellar, just pleasure if great and garish
losses can be consoled in the non-school of play.

After Mother's stroke

Those leaves unfold fans across the berm, sweet words seed her brain, imperfect thought shakes loose the native long unlearned. Even her daughter a breeze in the early plan she wants to shower with. A garden, a service station at the crossroads of recent breakdowns. Still, the signs are salty, the daikon press works same as the day it first tilted home. These pickles pin into her gift, days she gives bare reason for any next shelf. She's mollified the girl traps her spider of intent. A few grains of tea they force on each other, keep eyes' meet.

Worship (II)

Slow down the glassy minutes, I need to assemble angles of shine, the lapse between syllables they utter. Toss my scarf, a fence around edges, time's teeth seize the material, tired of transparency. Glass clinks against palpable.

I've arrived at moment, I feel like the host of a party. They flock around the scarf, the warmth is overwhelming. I find them something more to absorb, some tools they use to carve astounding crowns.

Orchestral pace. I remain in a central location. Sunflowers, heaven's constellations.

Discussions between sunrise and sunset, allowances, the everlasting clothes.

Approaching harvest

The pendulum still now, the center holds, I wait for you by the bank and you come. We console the sidewalk for its hard-heartedness and leave unsaddled by worry.

Bronze day, rung out by the bell tower. We choose *dazzle* over *wash the dishes*. I know you aren't schooled in village ways but I admire the way you don't blink when I use sassafras to cure my blues and music to iron out our ruffles.

I invite you to paddle upriver with me for how it feels to float the current down.

We bundle up for the barbecue in the backyard December first. It never snows here. We live among ripening kiwi, the unhunted pheasants crackle behind me down the alley.

Evidence

Frog on foot, glossy orange slipper on cloven hoof, electricity among city leaves. These cures.

Reside in harmonica and sea star, binoculars for circumspection.

The musician's wife wraps and wraps the practical wagon in snail shells until vertigo undoes intention. Gnats dart in stiffening air, lake's bulk accumulates a purple tablet.

I decide to be the experienced bride. Harmonics of orbit-change, perpetual repeat of the new.

Moments on the couch ambush gasps, it's no longer the heartbroken country western, no longer Edith Piaf's bravura lament. Trumpet is tuned to the orange-shoe shuffle. Most of us wear blue berets.

It isn't closing time. Just sunset and the provisional rocking boat.

Center of the mask

Unreeling words, can they lean far enough into her vertigo to transport her to the prismatic town, the new-prayer wheel? Prairie: a place to lie on her back in the dark on spring sod, watch constellations catch rides backwards into history's unspooling. "Thank you for the abandoned farmhouses," she says as she recounts yesterday's plucked chickens, stone soup. Good enough for night but not morning. She swore she'd be in Yosemite Valley to view its granite city rise into all that must pass without notice. The color green drills like a hornet's whine into her mind, the mind she garaged in the window-free ticking-down of days. No more pony rides, only the honeysuckle fragrant through the cracks in the boards, bits of light sifting in to spark her dormant desire.

Arrangement

Slip the blue silk wrap over the flannel pajamas, pretend the pattern of whorled shell mimes eyes' iridescence. What could a shell's consciousness be? She searches for covenants as her skin grows wens. More and more, she loves bed. Morning bubbles in light rain, hair still brown, she can carry the harvest sack. Nothing's too easy. Red in the tablecloth, hieroglyphic patterns decorate its borders. Some other person's reminiscence in her kitchen, maybe 1930. Eons. Shells, made of star matter. Her own bones. Some future artist, arranging the found femur, the seven vertebrae on sprays of honeysuckle, long tubes both sucked sweetness from, when young.

The untitled

Is it my birthday when the halo bursts? During nervous titterings, I
lace up blood, stanch gold shards with salt, but mending's no longer
on sale. A glum tilt persists, the bees' racket intense. We human
beings count on multiplication tables, set up aquariums on the back
lawn but mostly we huddle in mongrel outposts, building facades on
our three-car garages.

Nudge him awake, the partial provocateur, get him to write the
mystery he says will guarantee the bargain. I remember the children's
gratitude sprawled over cement that surrounds the swimming pool.
We parched adults, our gimlet-eyed spins in darkening twilight, reside
in June's better intent.

Union

Three pomegranates left on the tree, cracked, dribble knots of glassine kernels rich as late November's leftover sunlight. Willows stream-side will-lessly release their last yellow leaves. I think of the way winter forces the stripped willow withes to burnish nakedness to the same drenched red as these kernels pulling my hand to harvest. No lean fashion statement, but a calamity of overblown color, heat of my lover's skin, my ardent yes.

The Inadvisable

The critical process

There is this shadowed building I might enter. There is this yellow red road crossing into lawn, trees greener than common. I think of Van Gogh, his plummet into color. An untended bridge over the sketched-in river, too many glass panes to choose from. Whose life shall I mime today, how manage to continue to coax my teeth to shine—did Van Gogh worry when his fell out, were his moments one long worry? How to see through his blasphemous mind. Where in the picture to put my inner organs, their avid clashes, my inability to believe in them at all. I should take down the ladder to the attic, forget about unveiling the face of pharaoh, embalmed I suppose precisely in the hope of such immortal encounter. Vincent, you and I just want to get our pots of color set out if it takes us all day. And those crows and that corn, their perjury of importance equal to any pharaoh. Merriment of stars and how to make sure blue and yellow don't mix in the hard-to-see dark.

Reveal

Could I please open the sea? A package I've received, a friend sent it knowing my penchant for the grotesquely beautiful—the Flower Hat jelly fish, the giant sea turtle by moonlight in humped gleam, the shadows of pelicans wavering over the water. I wait for fossils of the sea lily to form, wait for coral to scar submerged rock. I leave my outpost by the wolf-spider's web, dew's vigor diminishing in the spongy August sun. I contemplate the summer décor of the scarlet/gold Sally Lightfoot crab; she's arranged herself fashionably on the black volcanic sand. Beach of nowhere, it's taken me weeks to paddle here, through kelp, praying to primeval fecundity. I'm a derelict oceanographer, to wait until I'm sixty-eight to immigrate into the banded iron deposits of Australia. I could have stuck with Hawai'i, its sooty terns and silversword, but I caught hummingbird fever and had to find the protea of South Africa, visit the night birds—Kakap and Kiwi—of New Zealand.

Gated

"Here," she hands me my ticket to the iris beds, our government's rein on wildness. I peer through privilege's keyhole, I've paid back my precise earned tax credit, I can climb into the zeppelin that will carry me over outlaws who own no credible mansion. Drifting through the ethos of *belong*, my camera prepares to snapshot the allowable. No *maybe* here, no unclipped rudimentaries. I shove under the seat belt my desire to remove my stockings, my palms have been squirted with a solution that zaps unwarrantied critters, bewildered in their ex-native habitats. No service without golf shoes, I've ditched my fondness for what gardeners call weeds, those old plant names spelled without capital letters, loose seeds lifting gossamer chins to the uncontrollable shapes of the moon.

Attempted escape or: The artist speaks

He's here again, the blond man in royal blue, it's the 70's and we're embracing color as never before. I'm wearing my would-be toga though I don't know why. I worry about champagne stains. We took the LSD with breakfast and the beach. We didn't realize emptiness would afford no guarantee of safety; after all, we're talking about our minds. I suppose that's the reason I thought the toga would be appropriate, a lot of lying down seemed inevitable, a sheet on the beach. I wore pajamas underneath. My beach togs, my beads. Everyone wears beads, some are red jade, for the healing of broken hearts, the man in the blue suit, the man in the bright red smoking jacket, other persons who are younger than most of us, what did we think we'd escape? Snakes around the ankles, feathers in the hair, linear thinking has given us wrong answers, broken storm cellars. This bleak architecture is all off. Pardons fly out of your hand, oh blue-coated man. I know you from some small-town corner in New York City, where together we painted out that horrible smoke-gray racket. We put up arbors, wisteria, visits to the Rockies during the brief, brief summer. We're entering the slipping down of 3:00 P.M.

Un-fortune

A wing to dislodge carpet and its vacuum cleaner. Air's rush kisses the meeting where nothing's decided, kicks out the crimson suspenders in charge. Shacks, beer, oyster shells become conversation's cargo, poker players in the eleventh-hour game.

That saying about unhitched in empty space without the glue that tries to hold genders together.

A fellow in a mustard-colored coat hands a fan to a high-heeled prick, everyone's supposed to hunch away from need in order to confess to society matrons. Better, suggest the scuttling of preconceived recipes, the pit concealed in cherries jubilee, sassy burning of librettos and funeraries.

Unlatch all political barbecues, lunch will be served off toast points. Something clicks out of place.

Sketches

I want the cosmos to grow from seeds I plant, thin as eyelashes dropped through sky's tunnel instead of caught in the plastic packet I buy from the nursery.

Cosmos flowers scratch my itch for significance, they're round as pinwheels, their stamens arrow into creation's gate.

Elsewhere grow the hybridized marigold's petals, ruffled like the frizzed hair some poor widow adopts, hoping for added reward, princely stranger to empty her closet drawers.

Marigolds, proverbial blondes elected to embellish the cultural myth.

Cosmos flowers simple as skulls, single layer, petal adjunct petal until a circle spreads edges into space.

Promises nailed into my viewing mind, sighing for a kind word, for the unpacked lunch.

Monday through Wednesday

Oh confident city where…
James Tate

Fishing rods unreeling in tandem commit themselves in feathered array to interpret the history of dance.

Milliners fake pears for bicycle-riders' fashion, they've called for revivals in Smith's barn. Monday over midair acrobats' restraining order.

Half the musicians are plucked guitar strings, poppies appear nightly, hornets wear gold shoulders, their stingers, swords that slumber.

Oh bulging village where sprinklers grow sunflowers to block driveways.

Who crosses the funeral's itinerary with whispers of crows in their cups?

Oh crowning town where citizens-for-unharming strike sparks in the band's rendition of "Beware the unbare harmony."

Unpack

Filter my body's juices through the cliff's drop, I remember where the orchard was cleaved in half by flooding waters, a sheaf of radiant blossoms besieged on the current's surface. No one can stop the raucous water skittering ruminantly into the clay we hoped would hold. It's not caress nor rage, it doesn't mirror the fundamental terror in the human marrow—it's what's beyond us that, still, we're part of. Weather. The fallback social subject matter, matters fundamentally to everyone, won't befuddle even a snake that knows precisely when to abandon the open path and take shelter. I admit it's the sky king, admit I need refuge, I loved those blossoms and apricots.

Remedy

When the new music comes in the enigmatic mail, how much grabs our absent December, shakes fluency from its desiccation, reconciles end with begin?

Begin with the flawed riot, rakish remedy for too much not-enough, simple breakfast that counters acquisition. Many bouffant petticoats forego skin-to-skin.

Skin refracts approach, or the blind puerile stagger. Hand held up/ hand beckoning. Memory of the face in the dark a moonish glow.

Laughter as though from music's middle.

Then there's warmth.

April

Paradise is full of foolishness.
Rumi

A plump heartbeat, a blue-glazed tower, tendrils sunk deeper than thought can yank out. Original, the human urge to open Pandora's box, no argument can stop. I strut in loosened wish-garb, I rush to become the charlatan poet, I hide myself from myself, reeling like a youth pealing with new nakedness. What holds a candle to choosing the inadvisable? Try to hypnotize that snake, drive so fast turning becomes swerve. My allotment: short toes, body for the savannah. I stretch to be more than myself, be rain, be a redwood tree, be the potter who makes the blue tower out of clay. Travel the subtle arterial maps to comprehend DNA. Be a fool for costume and heights.

Autumnal equinox

"Keep this, don't keep that." I sort through shelves of past experience, hoping for a future. Notice has been served, what supports me has to shift. Change the minutiae in my dreams. Venom I've milked and admired 'til my wires are corroded. Where to find a healthy urge to love without calculating the return? The acupuncturist reads my pulses, says, "Your liver's inflamed, you dwell in gall's region. I'm not one to tell you what to do, assuming you're here to improve, inhale mint and rub it...."

Once I was given rapture, I've been tracking it down ever since, but these deserts get in the way. Some arroyo, some flash flood, please. I'll leave my liver cruising through the mesquite, the cleansing aroma. Write it down on a tablet, every bitter thing I've tossed. Become a humiliated mendicant.

Beacon

A word glances off my teacher's cheek, sound's filament, a tiny tie between her mind and mine. No purposeful scroll, but strands where memory conjures and fumbles—we as mediums for myriad leaves. What else dangles just beyond sight? Some say concentric circles, existences I have not yet surrendered to. Futile, any wish I might employ to caress them into revelation. My foraging remains: to hold day in sight, coin earned from the game of the senses. Sit idle, feel time gather droplets against my skin. Let my teacher patrol the elusive limits, I'll borrow her shirt when I essay the journey.

Embrace

She does not forsake intense yellow, her particular village among locations the world offers. Yellow holds paramour, burnished morning, the ungrieving allegory that travel by foot provides.

She places fallible red beside it, echoes in her marrow, all she can't see crowds her shoulders, a cape not a shadow.

Black, born from bright and deep, signals *equivocal*, her hands muffled by the way night returns. She's accustomed to stars, their pause a series of question marks.

Nothing serene severs her from blood, her tread heavy in the gossamer field. Distance doesn't interest her, opening's nearby.

Birdcall calls her from sleep.

Holiday

Miserly of *reveal,* the forms lie sweetly in the stone, no tongue yet, no inked pen. I snatch the gleam as sun pokes down through leaves. Waxy smoothness hints at tooth, or flesh that wraps habit over bone.

Is meaning borrowed? Or is its abode the human vision of what might be coaxed? Imagination as virtue, or Devil's toy? But *play* be child's lesson and grown-up's *wash-away.* Dancing the axis, let mercy whirl like a saucy girl peeling off the orange rind to liberate scent.

This stone, uninhabited, is my neighbor. In it I read kite, snout, fingernail. It rises from its former funeral, offers me progeny: shades of rain, set moon's deep tones. Spread my picnic over its surface.

Loss in gain

Enchambered, encumbered, below the moon, above the shiny snail track, her hopes, luminous coins she refuses to spend. How many years has she rehearsed the new turn, never once lending a single coin to the day? "Shoulder responsibility," her mother exhorts from her workout. Blink and she'd fall, be rolled into her mother's bun, instantly anchored by hairpins. Why can't she use those coins, reminiscent of fresh air and mica flakes in river sand, washed and washed by shallow current? Remotely, she hears them sing. Her mother means her to settle for furniture. If she used them, would they disappear?

Unsaid

Curiosity steeps her in inquisitive tea. Questions: burrs or the way
the flesh of a cling peach won't release the pit. She knows it's her
love affair with the meaning of *begin*, but flesh must starve if seed
remain swathed.

Baroque night music. Her dreams topple the monument as it hoards
leftover light. She says, "Tear down the temple. Flush away form." Map
unwrites itself, ID card tears.

Darkness escapes the cul-de-sac, heals her bruised ego. She dresses
in Grandma's brocade curtains, plunges from the diving rope, listening
for accordions that swim her over rapids, Father fixed into a swing.

"Madam Camus"
  a painting by Edgar Degas

On the floor a hat box devoted to whim, freed from dress code, picture of a railway carriage, gesture toward the end of the track. Ruddy walls move forward, shawling her shoulders, lamp annoyingly neutral, unwilling to separate shadow from light. She wants crisp undressed air, October thumbing its nose at the backside days August wedges into summer's end. A quick escape out her side door before dinner would deny her silver brooch, pinned to her husband's right. He's absorbed in defining the meat from the bone. She comprehends the influence sun and moon exert over tree-climbing, the science of seafaring. She sits beautifully, dreams of ice-skating.

Portrait

The very large ear is the giveaway in the otherwise strict suit the man wears. It would seem I wish to hear the yaw and dwindle of earth to atom. His ear guarantees that I could speak from the other room of the hotel suite and not have to raise my voice, a thing I hate to do. But I couldn't evade his knowledge, I couldn't talk to myself. My secrets grow truculent, I begin to censor even thought, suspicious that the droll wrinkle his eyes express means he can read me. I don't know him well enough yet, I had a father. My silence becomes sheer fear even though it's no fluke I've conjured him in my life just when fame's starting its insistent roar. The red hair I've given him, the judgy clothes, bespeak a complexity I might invest in. Oh crossroads, recent rain, disappearance of urban frenzy, he and I together in the hotel albeit in separate rooms.

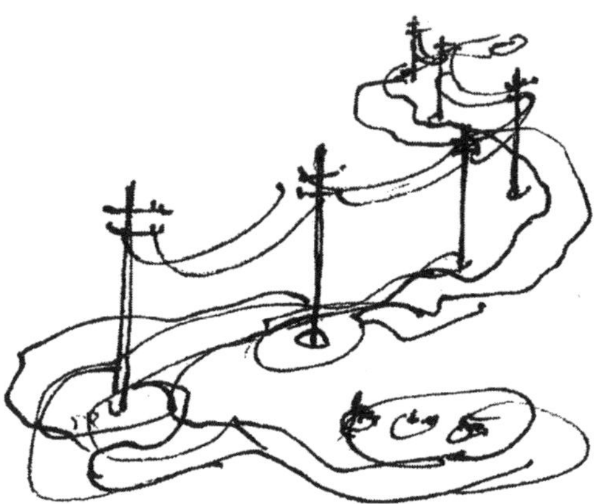

Guests

We thought camellias would be good companions until we understood they were foreign. We didn't make a scene but it's hard to find a girl or boy who's real. The gene pool on our recently annexed continent leans dangerously toward submission. In word and deed, serendipity lifts its daily barbells and contemplates the muddled universe within. Throwing out small-town duplicity, we shout down the parade route, we know how to dress for reception, to race desire for the clasp of song. On all the dirt roads left in America, native rabbits and ground squirrels lope, unafraid of amalgamated mouths ever increasing their speed like saviors along the sanctified highway.

"Thanatopsis"
       a painting by Joyce Treiman

Link arms with Death, what else can she do? He's been to call. He's
always hung just behind the door.

Paint roses twining up the sides, ask the horse to whinny and stomp
its blusterous way, but the rattle remains. It isn't breath, which still
belongs to her.

Since He's such a close relation (cousin, ancestor, familiar), why not
invite Him in? Horse sidesteps away, he must know Him too, 'though
to say *know* about the non-human mind can never be a sure thing.

It will be a different kind of banquet, since He doesn't eat. But she can
take the roses down from the door, bring in candles and the paintings
of Venice. Initiate the same old wordless conversation.

"Half Blood, Half Goddess"
                a sculpture by Lazlo Fekete

I could turn away but the stricken are still there.

Sweet roses with alabaster flesh. Yellow parsley, dandelion, small red rabbit under the goddess's knee. Easy to believe. I try to flirt with eternity but it blinks back disintegration. That's why I keep the pumpkin, collapsing with a puckered mouth, on the ledge outside my kitchen door.

My nation's president promulgates a generation of my students' deaths. Their blood will fast diminish into black filigree in soil far from home. Skull fragments lurk in sand to pierce future feet.

What does hatred look like? Not the action, but the snarl that burrs through the body?

Draw the circle complete, the Yin/Yang. Look through the small holes, black in white, white in black as though eyeholes in a mask. See the world: alabaster flowers in the rictus of mortal wound.

Kandinsky and symbolism

Before he leaves horses and the reach of their necks, he counts the visible landscape even at night. His eyes thicken perspective to trees, grass blades, birds tightly tucked. It isn't just forward, backward or sideways he wants, but to shave bald everything he's been taught, as though laughing were the same as flowing water. He knows it can't be the same water over the sixth stone from the bridge, it can't be the same roof seen hourly. He takes into account noon ripeness opposed to dawn green. The way horses' necks seem pillars of his childhood, leads him repeatedly to brilliance.

Author's biography

Grace Marie Grafton's poetry received first prize in the Bellingham Review contest and Nob Hill PEN Chapter, San Francisco, California. Her poems were a finalist for NIMROD's Pablo Neruda Prize and have twice been nominated for a Pushcart Prize. Her collection, *Zero*, won the Poetic Matrix Press chapbook contest. Her book, *Visiting Sisters*, published by Coracle Books, consists of poems inspired by the artwork of contemporary women.

She has taught for many years in the California Poets In The Schools program. For her teaching work, she has received numerous California Arts Council Artist In Residence grants. In 1998, she was named Teacher of the Year by the annual River Of Words youth poetry and art contest, co-sponsored by Robert Hass, former United States Poet Laureate.

She was born and raised on a grape farm near Reedley, in California's Central Valley. She earned a BA from the University of California, Berkeley and an MA from New York University, Manhattan. She lives in Oakland, California with her husband and extended family.